Life Without a Critical Spirit

Jim Hammer

Praise the Lord!

TEACH Services, Inc.
P U B L I S H I N G
www.TEACHServices.com • (800) 367-1844

World rights reserved. This book or any portion thereof may not be copied or reproduced in any form or manner whatever, except as provided by law, without the written permission of the publisher, except by a reviewer who may quote brief passages in a review.

The author assumes full responsibility for the accuracy of all facts and quotations as cited in this book. The opinions expressed in this book are the author's personal views and interpretations, and do not necessarily reflect those of the publisher.

This book is provided with the understanding that the publisher is not engaged in giving spiritual, legal, medical, or other professional advice. If authoritative advice is needed, the reader should seek the counsel of a competent professional.

Copyright © 2014 Jim Hammer
Copyright © 2014 TEACH Services, Inc.
ISBN-13: 978-1-4796-0386-2 (Paperback)
ISBN-13: 978-1-4796-0387-9 (ePub)
ISBN-13: 978-1-4796-0388-6 (Mobi)

All scripture quotations are taken from the New King James Version®.
Copyright © 1982 by Thomas Nelson, Inc. Used by permission. All rights reserved.

Published by

TEACH Services, Inc.
P U B L I S H I N G
www.TEACHServices.com • (800) 367-1844

Dedication

To all those who read my first book, *Victory Over a Critical Spirit*. To everyone who attended the camp meeting seminars I taught and encouraged me to write another book.

Introduction

After sharing my experiences in the book *Victory Over a Critical Spirit*, I felt impressed to continue the discussion and dig into the subject further, exploring what life would be like if we lived as Jesus did and distanced ourselves from a critical spirit.

As you prepare to read the insights I have been impressed with, consider these questions. What would it be like to live without the addiction of a negative, faultfinding, gossiping, and critical spirit? What would it be like to live a positive, peaceful, and uplifted life right here on earth? What does it feel like? What does it look like? Can we experience complete and lasting victory over a critical spirit? Is that victory necessary to have before Jesus returns?

Come journey with me through the following chapters as we examine life without a critical spirit. My prayer is that this will be a life-changing experience that will free you from every addiction—drugs, alcohol, sex, stealing, lying, cheating, gossiping, criticism, faultfinding, sarcasm—and sin that is separating you from Jesus, our Precious Lord and Savior.

Chapter 1

Possible or Not

I challenged you in *Victory Over a Critical Spirit* to take one hour (not while you're asleep) and not make one critical comment. If you have tried it and failed, keep trying; victory will come! All of heaven is in your corner. All of heaven is cheering for you. And all of heaven is doing EVERYTHING possible to save you. Paul likens this life to a race, yet we can all WIN the race! Praise the Lord that He not only runs the race with us but Jesus also gives us the grace, stamina, and encouragement to endure to the end.

You may think that living a life free from criticism, gossip, sarcasm, and negativity is too far reaching here on earth. You may even believe it is impossible. And it is if you try to do so in your own strength. But remember that with God *all* things are possible (Matt. 19:26). "Ah, Lord GOD! Behold, You have made the heavens and the earth by Your great power and outstretched arm. *There is nothing too hard for You*" (Jer. 32:17). Therein lies the key! A solid relationship with the I AM is necessary and vital for our spiritual well being. Without it we are doomed to a life of failure and final destruction.

Jesus experienced firsthand the difficulties and temptations of life on this earth, which is why, before His death, He prayed for you and me: "I do not pray for these alone, but also for those who will believe in Me through their word; that they all may be one, as You, Father, are in Me, and I in You; that they also may be one in Us, that the world may believe You sent Me. And the glory which You gave Me I have given them, that they may be one just as We are one." We have the privilege of *being one with God and each other*, but we must stay connected to Jesus and develop His character if we are to accomplish this goal.

Contemplate for a few moments what it would feel like to be free of any critical, negative, faultfinding thought or gossiping spirit toward another person for twenty-four hours. Try to imagine the peace of mind and stress-free comfort you would experience. Letting go of the negativity of life would improve your health and result in you waking up refreshed and regenerated, ready to start a new day with a Christlike Spirit. This picture is possible through the power of the Holy Spirit in our lives, transforming our minds one moment and one day at a time (Rom. 12:2).

Jesus wants to give us peace that "surpasses all understanding" (Phil. 4:7). All we have to do is allow Him to transform us into who He wants us to be. He promises that "He who has begun a good work in you will complete it" before He returns (Phil. 1:6). It's our decision! We can allow Jesus the freedom to change us and mold us to His character, or we can refuse and stay the way we are. What choice are you going to make?

Chapter 2

Do You Want to be a Jewel or a Stone?

"'They shall be Mine,' says the LORD of hosts, 'On the day that I make them My jewels'" (Mal. 3:17). The Lord wants to make us His jewels. He wants to refine us as gold, silver, and precious stones. He wants to mold us and transform us into His likeness. He wants to develop His character within us and make us into who and what He wants us to be. He longs to see His reflection when He looks at us. We can be jewels, polished and refined by God Himself, but we must allow Him to do His work and be cleansed by the blood of the Lamb.

When a raw diamond is found, it must be cleaned, cut, and polished before it becomes a precious stone of great value. Jewels are for special occasions and uses, such as the crown jewels of kings and queens and engagement and wedding rings. The Lord is preparing us, His children, for a special occasion too. He is refining us so that we will be ready for the wedding feast of the Lamb and eternity: "Let us be glad and rejoice and give Him glory, for the marriage of the Lamb has come, and His wife has made herself ready" (Rev. 19:7).

All of heaven is doing everything possible to find, clean, shape, and polish people in preparation for the kingdom of God. They are finding those who are searching for the truth and transforming them into God's likeness, polishing their characters, and preparing them to meet Jesus in the clouds of glory so that they may spend eternity with Him.

What we must remember is that it is *God's* work to transform us, not ours. Our job is to willfully submit to the transformation process and be a precious jewel instead of a stone. Think about it. Common stones are hard, course, and cold. They are difficult to shape and are used for everyday purposes. Gold, silver, and precious jewels, on the other hand, are easily melted, molded, and shaped.

Are our characters malleable and easily shaped by the Master Refiner? When He looks at us, does He see His reflection in us? Or does He see a common stone, one who is unwilling to be molded, has hard feelings, and is stiff-necked with a cold heart? Does He see someone whose words tear others down? Does He see someone who gossips and has a negative spirit? Does He see someone who seeks to judge and criticize others?

Do you want to be a precious jewel or a common stone? It is your decision. Will you allow the Holy Spirit to convict and convert you? Or do you want the enemy to shape your character? I realize that every human being has a critical spirit, but we do not have to remain that way. I also know that Jesus will never again allow a negative, critical, faultfinding, and gossiping spirit to enter heaven again. Lucifer was the first and last.

I believe with all my heart that even the heavenly angels are concerned about who the Lord will allow into heaven. They never again want to experience the lying, critical nature that Lucifer brought into God's kingdom. We only get a glimpse of the mental anguish Lucifer brought on the angelic host. Just think, a third of the angels were cast out of heaven. The heavenly angels lost some of their dearest friends and companions—what a heartbreaking experience that must have been for them. The rebellious angels chose a life of misery, turmoil, hardship, and wickedness, and in the end they will perish and be destroyed forever when God sets up the New Jerusalem.

I often wonder why anyone would choose to follow Satan down the destructive spiritual, mental, emotional, and physical path that he seeks to lead the world down, but many choose to wander after him, which is the free choice that God has given each person. However, we don't have to follow Satan. We can be free of his influence if we turn our lives over to God. The turmoil and aggravation that a critical spirit brings, which Satan seeks to keep alive in us, can be eliminated from our lives with God's help. Remember, "if we confess our sins, He is faithful and just to forgive us our sins and cleanse us from all unrighteousness" (1 John 1:9). When temptation comes, and it will, the Lord will give us the strength to overcome. He wants to deliver us from all the negative baggage of sin so that we can look at others through His eyes.

Chapter 3

Convicted by the Holy Spirit

Jeremiah aptly wrote that "the heart is deceitful above all things, and desperately wicked; Who can know it? I the LORD, search the heart, I test the mind, even to give every man according to his ways, according to the fruit of his doings" (Jer. 17:9, 10).

I often hear people say, especially when they know they are doing wrong, "The Lord knows my heart." Yes, He does know our hearts, and He knows that our hearts are desperately wicked. For this reason it is important to follow the promptings of the Holy Spirit. He will impress us as to what is really in our hearts, in the deep dark recesses, and He will show us how and what we need to do to transform our heart.

I was recently impressed by the Holy Spirit to speak to a certain man about how I had disrespected him some thirty years ago. I hadn't seen him for years, but I immediately prayed, "Lord, if you want me to seek forgiveness from this man, bring him to me." Well, within a matter of days, I was at a place of business, and when I came out, there he was, about ten feet from me, sitting in his truck. I was so ashamed that I could not even look at him.

Again two weeks later, I ran into him again at the grocery store. He was within one foot of me, but I pretended not to even notice him. When I left the store, I walked right in front of his truck with him sitting in it waiting for me to pass. Three times the Lord brought this man to me, and three times I failed to do what the Holy Spirit wanted me to do. Although I prayed the same prayer for months after these encounters, the Lord did not bring him to me again.

Every day I wrestled with the thought that I had failed and that I still needed to make things right with this man. I continued to pray, but this time it was a different prayer. This time I prayed that the Holy Spirit would not leave me. Like King David, in Psalm 51:11, I prayed, "Do not take Your Holy Spirit from me." I also prayed that the Holy Spirit would trouble me day and night until this matter was rectified.

After months of struggling with this issue, I decided to go to his house and seek forgiveness and accept whatever the Lord's will was for this situation. At long last, I was at peace. When the Holy Spirit convicts us of sin or of something we need to address, we need to respond to the conviction in a positive way. There is no doubt in my mind that He will convict us of everything that will hinder our salvation, including a critical, negative, and sarcastic spirit.

This experience may seem trivial or of little consequence since it happened so many years ago, but it was one of the most difficult situations I have ever had to face, for I continued to wrestle with it to the point that I feared the Holy Spirit would leave me, which would have had eternal consequences. In the end, I determined that spending eternity with my Precious Savior and following the prompting of the Holy Spirit was more important than my pride or my fear of what would happen when I confronted this man with my past sin.

Paul writes in 1 Timothy 4:1, 2: "The Spirit expressly says that in latter times some will depart from the faith ... speaking lies in hypocrisy, having their own conscience seared with a hot iron." The Holy Spirit communicates with us through our conscience, but He cannot impress a conscience that has been scorched and that is unwilling to listen.

The Holy Spirit will bring to our minds the things that are separating us from Jesus. Like the hymn says, "Nothing between my soul and my Savior." As we allow Him to search our hearts, there will be cleansing of all our unrighteousness, so we can be filled with the Lord's righteousness (1 John 1:9; Isa. 54:17).

The Holy Spirit will impress each one concerning the heart issues that need to be made right, not only with each other, but also with the Lord. The Holy Spirit knows our thoughts more than we do. The Lord is anxious to heal us. He longs for us to lay our burdens upon Him and leave them there. Don't be like Jonah; don't run from God. There is nowhere you can we go to hide from God. He is everywhere! From the highest of heights to the lowest depths of the earth, He is there.

If you want peace that surpasses all understanding, ask the Holy Spirit to reveal to you what is in your heart, and then allow Him to help you make things right. When you do that, peace will come! When we submit our will to the Holy Spirit and let Him refine us, our thoughts and words will be transformed, and our homes and churches will be blessed.

Chapter 4

But I'm Only Human

Our struggle with sin is a constant battle we must wage. King David understood this struggle well, and he cried out to God: "Cleanse me from secret faults. Keep back Your servant also from presumptuous sins; let them not have dominion over me.... Let the words of my mouth and the meditation of my heart be acceptable in Your sight, O Lord, my strength and my Redeemer" (Ps. 19:12-14). If we are to overcome sin, we need to ask God for help and rely on His strength to conquer the sins in our lives.

Jesus communed with His Father and relied on Him to help Him through every moment of every day. This special relationship with His Father continued to shine through in Jesus' attitude toward others, which was one of love, kindness, sympathy, and a burden for the lost souls of men. When He rebuked people, He did so with a breaking heart, with a desire for one's salvation, and with a spirit of love, a spirit that was willing to die for them. If we are to overcome sin, we must emulate the life of our Saviour.

There is an acronym that became popular a number of years ago—WWJD, which stands for "What Would Jesus Do?"—that reminds us to think about how Jesus would handle everyday temptations and challenges. Jesus is our leader, our example, our pattern, our model. And yet, so many are still trying to do things their way in their own power, and they are falling flat on their face. Is it because we have not FULLY SURRENDERED our hearts to the Lord? Or is it possible that we may have other gods in our lives?

We are standing on the very shore of eternity! Victory is within our grasp; Jesus has already provided it for us. There is not one temptation that comes our way that a way of escape has not already been provided (1 Cor. 10:13). I personally believe the Lord provides multiple avenues of escape, which means that we can either choose the temptation or the avenue of escape and freedom from sin. It's our decision! Paul writes through the anointing of the Holy Spirit that "sin shall not have dominion over you, for you are not under law but under grace" (Rom. 6:14). Paul also stated that "where sin abounded, grace abounded much more" (Rom. 5:20). This does not mean we should sin to receive more grace or that we should disregard the laws of God. Simply put, God will shower us with so much grace that we don't have to sin.

Many people use the excuse that they are only human and they can't avoid sinning. What a cop out. Enoch and Elijah were only human too, but they were translated. Look at Moses, Joseph, and Daniel who were also humans. What God did for them and through them He will do for us because "Jesus Christ is the same yesterday, today, and forever" (Heb. 13:8).

We need to allow the Holy Spirit to show us the sins in our own lives instead of focusing our attention on the faults of others. It is so much easier to point fingers at other people than to examine our own deficiencies. There is enough sin in our own lives to be concerned about that we shouldn't look for the sins in someone else's life. And isn't that the Holy Spirit's work anyways? So often we want to usurp His authority, but we need to leave things in God's hands. For when we don't, we are falling into Satan's trap. "Satan exults over the conditions of God's professed people. While many are neglecting their own souls, they eagerly watch for an opportunity to criticize and condemn others" (White, *Testimonies for the Church*, vol. 5, p. 95). Imagine what our lives would be like if we looked at our own lives instead of looking at other people. Oh what peace we often forfeit, only because we take our eyes off of Jesus. How sad!

Victory will only come through much prayer and a constant connection with the Lord. "It is by constant, unceasing effort that we maintain the victory over the temptations of Satan" (White, *Testimonies for the Church*, vol. 3, p. 253). In *Patriarchs and Prophets*, we read, "God made such ample provision that man need never have been defeated in the conflict with Satan" (White, p. 332). *Ample provisions have been made* that we never need to fall into temptation. The enemy never has and never will ensnare God. God has already made preparations for every plan of the enemy so that we are not overcome. Only through our faithful connection with Jesus are we secure. This will prevent the enemy from snatching us out of the hand of God. We serve such an awesome, precious God!

The Lord wants us to have freedom from tension and stress in our life. We just need to trust the Lord and ask Him to free us from the chains of criticism that bind us. Pray as if your life is dependent upon it, because it is. Without a constant connection with God and the throne of grace, we will be defeated.

Chapter 5

Humble or Humiliated

Nowhere in Scripture have I read where God will humble us, but I have read where He has humiliated many—Cain, Aaron and Miriam, Haman, Job's three friends, King Nebuchadnezzar, and Paul on the road to Damascus. We can do what Scripture admonishes and humble ourselves before the Lord, or we can continue to allow our pride to be the lord of our lives, and in the end, be humiliated and possibly lost.

Jesus humbled Himself when He became a human being and agreed to live on this fallen planet (Phil. 2:8). He willingly succumbed to the trials of this life for us. Whatever cruel treatment we experience, we will never experience what Jesus went through. Jesus is everything; He is the King of glory, the First and Last, the Alpha and Omega, the Bright and Morning Star, the Beloved of the Father, our Rock and Savior, and the Prince of Peace, and that's only a small list of attributes that describe Him.

Even with all of these titles, He came to live here with us! That kind of love is beyond my comprehension. And yet He loves us that much, and He calls us to love others in the same way that He loves us. Jesus calls us to humble our hearts and take up our cross daily (Luke 9:23). As we do so, all the things that are not of Christ will fall away from us and our character will change and become more Christlike.

"The Spirit Himself bears witness with our spirit that we are children of God" (Rom. 8:16). Isn't it time to conduct ourselves as children of the King? If we truly believe we are the King's children, and I do, then we need to act like princes and princesses of the heavenly court. We need to demonstrate the fruit of the Spirit in our lives, that of love, joy, peace, longsuffering, kindness, goodness, faithfulness, gentleness, and self-control. This can only be achieved as we submit and commit our minds and bodies to Christ as Paul calls us to do: "Present your bodies a living sacrifice, holy, acceptable to God, which is your reasonable service" (Rom. 12:1). When we submit to Christ, "He who has begun a good work in you will complete it until the day of Jesus Christ" (Phil. 1:6).

Paul states that we should esteem others as better than ourselves. If we would look at each other in the light of Paul's counsel, there would be a taste of heaven on earth. We will discover peace and happiness as we allow the Lord to strip us of our sinful pride, making our homes and churches a safe place for people to share their burdens and support one another in love. Our focus has to change from criticizing one another to loving one another. When we criticize, we hinder the Holy Spirit's prompting, not allowing Him to convict and convert. We need to get out of the Holy Spirit's way so that He can bring His people to repentance. This is especially needed in our homes. The ones we love the most are the ones we hinder spiritually. We would see amazing changes in our spouses and children if we loved them as Jesus loves them.

Let me encourage you to do whatever you have to do to make your home a place of encouragement and gracious love, which is what Jesus wants it to be. What joy and peace of mind we will have when we follow God's plan!

Chapter 6

A Taste of Heaven

There is so much turmoil in the world, and in many cases the turmoil is in our own lives. Stress is ever present. Families are being torn apart. Children are bounced from place to place. Spirituality is on the decline. Negativism is running unrestrained. There is a lack of concern for the feelings of others. Homes appear to be playgrounds, and the main focus is not on Christ, who alone gives true happiness and healing. We try to give our children good gifts, but how many of us offer them the best gift, a loving, lasting, meaningful, and saving relationship with Jesus Christ.

Is this possible? Yes! When our children are young, the training needs to be Christ-centered and focused on heaven. From infancy to childhood, through the teenage years and adulthood, our lives must model that of Christ. Many of us make a big mistake when we preach to our children, especially our adult children, instead of letting our lives reflect Christ and praying that He work upon their hearts. It is our job to pray; it is the Holy Spirit's job to convict.

If your home is not Christ-centered, it is never too late to make a change. The Lord will help you transform your home and family into what He desires it to be. Pray earnestly that the Lord's desires will become your desires and that your home will be as Ellen White described. "It [home] should be a little heaven on earth, a place where the affections are cultivated instead of being studiously repressed. Our happiness depends upon this cultivation of love, sympathy, and true courtesy to one another. The sweetest type of heaven is a home where the Spirit of the Lord presides. If the will of God is fulfilled, the husband and wife will respect each other and cultivate love and confidence" (*The Adventist Home*, p. 15).

The Lord desires that the love for each family member be the type of love He has for us. He desires that our homes should be a haven of rest, safety, and security. Our homes should be filled with joy, happiness, and peace. Consistently, our homes should be a place where Jesus is the center of everything. This may sound like an impossible goal, but with God all things are possible. The only thing usually hindering the fulfillment of this type of home is the pride that is exhibited by its residents. And that's the root of all our problems. The critical, negative, faultfinding, and proud spirit really takes root where Christ is not allowed to dwell.

The home where Christ dwells will declare a moratorium on a critical, negative spirit, and if this type of behavior does arise, those involved will be fast to apologize for a word spoken in anger or haste, fast to show the love of God to each other. When this type of behavior is cultivated in our homes, it will spill out and extend to our church family and community. Oh what peace of mind we would experience!

Let me remind you about how this can be accomplished. Only through Christ can there be victory! Only through sincere prayer can a personal connection with Him be sustained, which will translate into the development of positive relationships with those around us. Every aspect of life is affected for the better if we maintain a close relationship with our Lord and Savior. Although this may seem impossible, remember that "I can do all things through Christ who strengthens me" (Phil. 4:13).

Do you want all of Jesus? Actually, the question should be, does He have all of you? Oh what a peaceful and less stressful life we would experience, right here on earth, if we gave ourselves completely over to the will of God. Do you want a peaceful life? Do you want a life without stress? Do you want a worry-free life? In the book *Thoughts from the Mount of Blessings*, Ellen White wrote, "He who is at peace with God and his fellow men cannot be made miserable. Envy will not be in his heart; evil surmising will find no room there; hatred cannot exist. The heart that is in harmony with God is a partaker of the peace of heaven and will defuse its blessed influence on all around" (p. 28). Christ's followers are sent into the world with a message of peace. A message of reconciliation!

Do you want to live a life that is not controlled by what others say or do? Nelson Mandela, after spending twenty-seven years in prison, made this statement, "As I walked out the door toward the gate that would lead to my freedom, I knew if I did not leave my bitterness and hatred behind, I'd still be in prison."

We must concentrate on what the Lord said and did when dealing with difficult people and challenging situations. Make Jesus Lord of your life, and let Him have all of you—your heart, your mind, your very being. When you do that all bitterness will leave you. Nothing that anyone has done to us can compare to what we have done to Jesus.

In this journey called life, we can't look backwards and expect to go forward. The enemy wants to keep us locked in our past mistakes and way of life, but Jesus wants to transform us and take us into the future and into eternity. Keep your focus on the high calling that is in Christ, and remember that our tongues need to be bridled! The few pages that comprise the book of James are an excellent transcript of the Lord's plan for our relationships.

Remember, you can create a home that is a taste of heaven right here on earth.

Chapter 7

Almost Home

Imagine that we are on the heavenly shores, ready to cross into the Promised Land of eternity. All differences have been put away. Every critical and negative spirit is gone. There is no more sarcasm. There is no gossiping, no undermining of plans, nothing that would cause dissention, no deception or cunning spirit. There will be complete harmony, and unity will prevail at last.

Jesus, the Prince of Peace, calls us to be peacemakers, not peace breakers, here on earth, and when we follow His plan, we'll be blessed and be a blessing to others. We are heirs of our heavenly Father, and our inheritance is heaven itself. As heirs, we need to prepare for life in the kingdom of God. We need to cultivate the habit of speaking well of others. We need to dwell on the good qualities of those we associate with and minimize their errors and failings. When we are tempted to complain about what others have said or done, we need to find something to praise them for. We need to cultivate a spirit of thankfulness. As ambassadors of Christ, we have no time to dwell on the faults of others. Evil speaking really effects more heavily the speaker than the hearer. "The very act of looking for evil in others develops evil in those who look" (White, *The Ministry of Healing*, p. 492).

Now is the time to prepare! Jesus has already paid for all of our faults and sins and has gained the victory for us. We need to reach out and take hold of it. Remember that the enemy is a defeated foe; he may win a few battles, but he has already lost the war. We are on the winning team. Paul likens it to participating in a race, and we all can be victorious. We can all wear a crown of glory (1 Cor. 9:24–27). Now is the time to decide whose team you want to be on. Do you want to be on the winning team or the defeated team?

Some time ago I had a dream. I dreamed I was in heaven walking on the streets of gold with another person. We noticed Jesus walking toward us, and when we met, I asked Jesus if we could sing for Him. He was so gracious as He listened to our song. When we finished, He said it was beautiful. Then He asked if He could sing for us? When I awoke, I contemplated the fact that I had never thought about Jesus singing before. Now I'm looking forward to hearing Him sing. I'm sure the melody will be sweet and tender with the most beautiful voice I have ever heard.

> The Lord your God is with you,
> He is mighty to save:
> He will rejoice over you with gladness,
> He will quiet you with His love,
> He will rejoice over you with singing.
>   Zephaniah 3:17

As we near our heavenly home, let's strive to make our earthly home as pleasant and happy as Jesus wants it to be.

Chapter 8

Home at Last

When Jesus returns the trumpet will sound, the faithful dead will rise, and we who are alive will join them and meet Jesus in the air (1 Thess. 4:16, 17). He will lift us up with a mighty hand and take us from this sinful planet to meet Him in the air. Just as He will guide us to Him in the clouds when He returns, He will guide us now on this earth if we will take the time to sit at His feet and tune our minds to Him.

When Jesus returns He will lead us into eternity and will joyously present us faultless before our heavenly Father (Jude 1:24). We will visit worlds unknown to us now. Way beyond our present galaxy, we will soar into the heavens, stopping at planets that we've never heard of.

Aside from the joy of exploring the universe, the very best part of heaven will be spending eternity with Jesus, our Savior and Redeemer, the One who paid such an expensive price for us. We are damaged goods, yet Jesus paid the full price for us. He snatched us out of the enemy's claws and delivered us from him. Oh, what a wonderful God we will worship and serve throughout eternity. Won't it be great to see Him face to face, to ask Him about the things that perplexed our minds while here on earth? I can't wait to embrace Him and feel His arms of love encircled around me.

No matter what we believe heaven will be like, we are told it will be even better than that. "Eye has not seen, nor ear heard, nor have entered the heart of man the things which God has prepared for those who love Him" (1 Cor. 2:9). It will be a zillion times better than any Christmas or vacation or event we've ever experienced.

There is no doubt in my mind that there is a giant celebration being planned for us. When we enter through the pearly gates and walk on the streets of gold, I'm sure the angelic choir will be there to sing songs of triumph and celebration. The Father, Jesus, and the Holy Spirit will embrace us in their trusting arms and exclaim, "Well done, good and faithful servants ... enter into the joy of your lord" (Matt. 25:21). Then Jesus will show us the mansions He has built for us (John 14:2). I believe our homes are already prepared, just waiting for us. Rooms made of gold, silver, diamonds, precious gems; walls of beautiful flowers; and magnificent landscapes with a view of the cosmos that extend for hundreds, maybe thousands of miles.

I also believe that there will be the most beautiful banquet, beyond what our eyes and palates have ever feasted on, prepared for the redeemed. The food will be exceptionally delicious and delicate, the most nutritious and finest fruits, nuts, and juices we have ever tasted or seen. We will drink pure crystal clear water from the river of life.

But most of all, no matter where we are seated, no matter how many miles long the table will be, we will be able to see Jesus, as if we were sitting right across from Him. Looking for and talking with our loved ones and friends is another joy we will experience. Everyone there will be part of the family of God. That joy will be indescribable too. Sharing the blessings and the trials, recalling all the hope and love that we received during our time on earth. We will also realize that everything we experienced was well worth the sacrifice, for the reward is beyond comprehension. I know we will exclaim, "Heaven is cheap enough."

We will experience such joy, for " God will wipe away every tear from their eyes; there shall be no more death, nor sorrow, nor crying. There shall be no more pain, for the former things have passed away" (Rev. 21:4)

Chapter 9

The Earth Made New

In Revelation 21:1 John "saw a new heaven and a new earth, for the first heaven and the first earth had passed away." John also saw the holy city, New Jerusalem, coming down out of heaven from God. The Old Testament book of Isaiah confirms the coming of a the new earth: "For behold, I create new heavens and a new earth; and the former shall not be remembered or come to mind" (Isa. 65:17).

According to the Word of God, after we spend a thousand years in heaven we will return to this earth to live for eternity. The earth will be made new, and we will be participants in all the wonders of the Lord. Isaiah 65:21 states that we will build houses and live in them. But what about the mansion that Jesus has built for us (John 14:1–4)? Will we have two dwellings, one in the city of the New Jerusalem and a country estate in the earth made new? I believe we will. Praise the Lord.

Isaiah 65:21 also says that we will "plant vineyards and eat their fruit." That means it will be a rather spacious estate with plenty of elbowroom. Our feeble minds have trouble grasping this picture. But it is just before us! You don't want to be left out. Hang on! We are so close to the return of our Savior. Keep the faith, and don't forsake the Lord.

If we want to live for eternity in the new earth, we must prepare ourselves now for the life to come. All of heaven and the worlds that have not fallen live in unity, and all of God's people on earth will have learned to live in the unity of heaven before Christ returns. So when Jesus takes us home, we will already be in harmony with the entire universe. We must be vigilant and guard our thoughts and words. What we read, what we look at, and what we think about determine our destiny. We must strive to be Christlike in all that we do and say. And with God's help, we will be victorious.

I want to encourage you to prepare yourself, through the power of the Holy Spirit, by perfecting your character here on earth, burying your critical spirit, and drawing closer to Jesus every day. Is it your heart's desire to follow Jesus? When He returns, are you confident that you will follow Him into eternity? Today is the first day of the rest of your life. Today is the day of salvation! Today is the day to make the most important decision you will ever make! Today is the day to ask Jesus to make you more like Him!

About the Author

Jim Hammer has been involved in ministry for twenty-five years, serving as a lay pastor for approximately four years, head elder for more than twenty years, and is currently the New York Conference prayer coordinator. Through the course of his time in leadership he has witnessed the destruction of churches that entertain a critical spirit and the restoration of churches that adopt Christ's character. He hopes that readers will "search their hearts to see if they are building their church up or tearing it down." Now retired, his greatest joy comes from spending time with his wife, children, and grandchildren.

Jim is passionate about helping others develop a positive spirit and a Christlike character. A member of the New York Conference of Seventh-day Adventists, he has presented seminars at camp meetings, prayer breakfasts, and at various churches throughout the New York Conference.

He is available as a guest speaker and presenter for church seminars, camp meetings, and church and/or conference retreats. Materials can be adapted for seminars and conferences in a secular setting as well. If you are interested in having Jim speak for an upcoming event, please contact him at 716-532-4099 or JHammer562@aol.com.

Bibliography

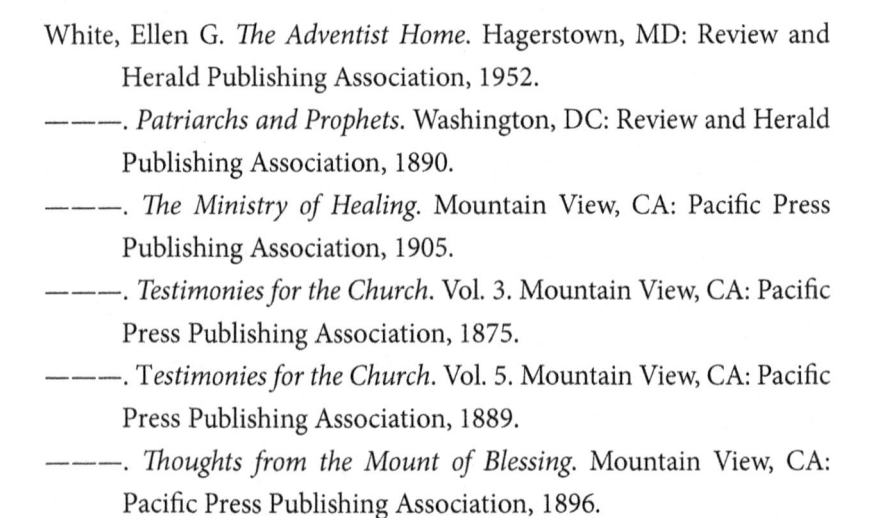

White, Ellen G. *The Adventist Home*. Hagerstown, MD: Review and Herald Publishing Association, 1952.

———. *Patriarchs and Prophets*. Washington, DC: Review and Herald Publishing Association, 1890.

———. *The Ministry of Healing*. Mountain View, CA: Pacific Press Publishing Association, 1905.

———. *Testimonies for the Church*. Vol. 3. Mountain View, CA: Pacific Press Publishing Association, 1875.

———. *Testimonies for the Church*. Vol. 5. Mountain View, CA: Pacific Press Publishing Association, 1889.

———. *Thoughts from the Mount of Blessing*. Mountain View, CA: Pacific Press Publishing Association, 1896.

We invite you to view the complete
selection of titles we publish at:

www.TEACHServices.com

Scan with your mobile
device to go directly
to our website.

Please write or e-mail us your praises, reactions, or
thoughts about this or any other book we publish at:

TEACH Services, Inc.
P U B L I S H I N G
www.TEACHServices.com • (800) 367-1844

P.O. Box 954
Ringgold, GA 30736

info@TEACHServices.com

TEACH Services, Inc., titles may be purchased in bulk for
educational, business, fund-raising, or sales promotional use.
For information, please e-mail:

BulkSales@TEACHServices.com

Finally, if you are interested in seeing
your own book in print, please contact us at

publishing@TEACHServices.com

We would be happy to review your manuscript for free.